LIGHT FROM DARK AGES?

AN EVANGELICAL CRITIQUE OF CELTIC SPIRITUALITY

D1569018

BY MARIAN RAIKES

The Latimer Trust

Light From Dark Ages? An Evangelical Critique of Celtic Spirituality
© Marian Raikes 2012

ISBN   978-1-906327-05-7

Cover photo: Celtic cross with blue sky © Martin Heaney–Fotolia.com

Published by the Latimer Trust January 2012

The Latimer Trust (formerly Latimer House, Oxford) is a conservative Evangelical research organisation within the Church of England, whose main aim is to promote the history and theology of Anglicanism as understood by those in the Reformed tradition. Interested readers are welcome to consult its website for further details of its many activities.

The Latimer Trust
London N14 4PS UK
Registered Charity: 1084337
Company Number: 4104465
Web: www.latimertrust.org
E-mail: administrator@latimertrust.org

CONTENTS

Introduction

The 'Dark Ages' (i.e. approximately the fourth to tenth centuries AD) are popularly considered a period of history about which people know little beyond the presumption that life was short and hard. Christianity, whether in or out of the monasteries, is often presented as a largely impersonal, formal religion – little more than the culture of the time. But is that a true picture? Or did 'the light of the glorious gospel of Christ' shine as brightly then as in other 'dark' periods of history? In particular, did it shine through the original Celtic version of Christianity in such a way that we may profitably imitate the Celtic Christians? And to what extent does it shine through the innumerable versions of the current revival of 'Celtic spirituality'?

That we are experiencing a 'revival' of professedly 'Celtic' spirituality is beyond doubt. There are 'Celtic' fonts and 'Celtic' recipes, 'Celtic' poems and 'Celtic' websites galore. There are shops stocking 'Celtic' jewellery, cards, and craftwork. There are bookshelves laden with anthologies of 'Celtic' prayers and CDs of 'Celtic' music. There are organised 'pilgrimages' to 'Celtic' places like Iona and Lindisfarne. Iona, for example, reputedly attracts some 250,000 visitors a year. So, why this phenomenal interest in all things 'Celtic'?

A wide range of explanations have been suggested, of which the following six seem to have achieved some degree of consensus among writers on the subject. They are, in no particular order.

1)   The years between the fourth and tenth centuries in Celtic lands are perceived by many to have been some sort of spiritual 'golden age'; an age when a people living on the fringes of the then known world were free to experience an 'authentic' Christianity untainted by the corruptions of Roman 'civilisation.' Culling

expresses it well: "It is presented as a lost ideal, a missed opportunity... awaiting recovery in our own day."[1]

2)   Interest in all things Celtic is seen as one expression of a generation seeking to recover its roots and to establish its identity in our fragmented postmodern world. Esther De Waal, for example, speaks of her explorations into Celtic spirituality taking her "back to the part of myself that is more ancient than I am, and this is of course the power of the Celtic heritage."[2]

3)   Because the spiritual roots which many seek and find in Celtic Christianity are pre-iconoclast and pre-Reformation, they are highly valued as a foundation for ecumenism.[3] Several writers therefore hail the revival of Celtic Christianity as 'a way forward', a way for the denominations to work together, even a way to possible reunification.[4] Consider, for example, Michael Mitton's testimony:

> As a Protestant I had never felt entirely comfortable with finding my spiritual roots in the religious and political protests of the sixteenth century, particularly as I am good friends with a number of Roman Catholics and have a great respect for their church... here, in the Celtic church, there are common roots that go back long before our days of separation.[5]

4)   The 'nature' poetry of Celtic monks, often combined with some dubious modern theology concerning creation, has resulted in

---

[1] Elizabeth Culling, *What is Celtic Christianity?* (Bramcote: Grove Spirituality Series 45, 1993), p 4.
[2] Esther De Waal, *The Celtic Way of Prayer: The Recovery of the Religious Imagination* (London: H&S, 1996), p 2.
[3] See, eg, Donald Meek, 'Modern Celtic Christianity: The Contemporary 'Revival' and its Roots', *SBET* 10 (1992) p 21.
[4] See eg Ray Simpson, *Celtic Spirituality: Rhythm, Roots and Relationships* (Cambridge: Grove SS 85, 2003), p 5; De Waal, *The Celtic Way of Prayer*, p 3; Michael Mitton, *Restoring the Woven Cord: Strands of Celtic Christianity for the Church Today* (London: DLT, 1995), p 2.
[5] Mitton, *Restoring the Woven Cord*, p 1f.

Celtic spirituality being labelled 'green.' It tends therefore to prove very attractive to anyone interested in ecology and the environment.

5)   Many adherents of Celtic spirituality today claim that a large part of the attraction is in its alleged tolerance, feminism and lack of dogmatism or institutionalism.

6)   Celtic spirituality is also commonly perceived as more holistic, down-to-earth, non-cerebral and in touch with human feelings than other Christian traditions. Thus it proves attractive to many Christians (including evangelicals) who find themselves longing for a more experientially satisfying relationship with God. As the back cover of the *Celtic Resource Book* assures them:

> Celtic Christianity... is a living tradition waiting for you to enjoy, breathe in and find your own soul enriched. Whatever your spiritual background... this is not about replacing it with something new: it is about a resource to take you deeper...[6]

Whatever the reason for the attraction in any specific instance, many proponents believe the current revival of 'Celtic' spirituality can bring nothing but the greatest benefit to the church. Michael Mitton says, for example: "For Britain, the period from the fifth to ninth centuries should be seen as the 'Light Ages' where arguably a light shone that has been brighter than any since."[7]   He is not alone in his view; it is shared not only by individuals such as Esther De Waal and Ian Bradley but by whole communities such as the Community of Aidan and Hilda, based on Lindisfarne, or the Iona community, of which more later.

Meanwhile, before we turn to consider the literature under discussion, and the distinctive features of Celtic spirituality in both its original and contemporary forms, we must address a few preliminary questions.

---

[6]   Martin Wallace *The Celtic Resource Book* (London: Church House Publishing, 1998)
[7]   Michael Mitton, *Restoring the Woven Cord*, p 2.

3

What is 'Spirituality'?

'Spirituality' is often described as a 'slippery' term and it is notoriously difficult to define. Many evangelicals are understandably wary of it, being as it is a 'synthetic theological construct' not directly taken from the Bible.[8] There are a number of biblically valid definitions (and even more invalid ones!). For our present purposes, I intend to use one of the simplest definitions, namely that 'spirituality' is 'the way people practice what they believe.' In other words, biblical spirituality works "outward from a central core of biblical theology,"[9] just as any non-biblical spirituality will ultimately work outward from a core of non-biblical theology, even if that is not always immediately apparent. Therefore this booklet will consider the distinctives of Celtic Christian theology before its spirituality.

Was there ever a 'Celtic church'?

The original Celts were both geographically and culturally diverse, including, for example, Irish, Welsh and Bretons. Their culture was tribal, and they would not have identified themselves as one race. Nor was there ever one organised Celtic church. As a result, there is much debate over whether it is valid and meaningful to speak of 'Celtic Christianity' at all.

As O'Loughlin points out, "The term 'Celtic' was coined by philology to express common characteristics of a language-family... There never was a 'Celtic' rite, much less a 'Celtic' church,"[10] and

---

[8]   For those who wish to consider the problems of 'Spirituality' further, Don Carson has written a very helpful article: Carson, D.'When is spirituality spiritual? Reflections on some problems of definition' in *Journal of the Evangelical Theological Society* 37/3, Sept 1994, pp 381-394. This article has since been reprinted as an appendix in the back of *The Gagging of God* (Grand Rapids: Zondervan, 1996).

[9]   Carson, D.'When is spirituality spiritual?' in *The Gagging of God,* p 567

[10]   Following the Welshman Edward Lloyd (*Archaeologia Britannica*, 1707) languages commonly accepted as belonging to the Celtic family are: Irish, Welsh, Scottish, Gaelic, Manx, Cornish, Breton and Gaulish.

Celtic theologians "saw themselves belonging to a single religious body", periodically involving themselves with continental monasteries and schools. The main differences were to do with liturgy and doctrinal expressions."[11] Thus he rejects any suggestion of one consistent spirituality across the Christian Celts.

However, there are undoubtedly similarities in approach to Christian theology and spirituality among the various 'Celtic' groupings. So most writers now conclude, with Allchin, that "there is such a thing as Celtic Christianity,"[12] even if the label 'Celtic' is somewhat arbitrary. In this booklet, I use the term 'Celtic' simply to refer to people whose first language was one of the Celtic ones.

Are the sources reliable?

The study of Celtic Christianity has always suffered from a paucity of reliable sources. The general rule is that the later the source, the less reliable it is likely to be, and unfortunately, relatively little has survived from before the mid-seventh century. Furthermore, much contemporary 'Celtic' spirituality looks back, not so much to original Celtic material, as to that coming from the nineteenth century revival of interest, which was heavily influenced by romanticism and antiquarianism.[13]

As a result, many academics have become frustrated with popular books produced by 'Celtic' enthusiasts, claiming that, because the authors have relied on poor translations and secondary sources, their conclusions are misleading.

---

[11] Thomas O'Loughlin, "Celtic Spirituality" in *The New SCM Dictionary of Spirituality* (London: SCM, 2005), p 183

[12] A.M. Allchin, "There is no Resurrection where there is no Earth: Creation and Resurrection as seen in early Welsh poetry" in M. Atherton *Celts and Christians: New Approaches to the Religious Traditions of Britain and Ireland* (Cardiff: University of Wales, 2002), p 103

[13] Especially to Alexander Carmichael's *Carmina Gadelica*; see chapter 5

Donald Meek, for example, protests that the depictions of many Celtic saints are so dressed up in contemporary garb that they scarcely resemble the real Celtic saints.[14]

And J.R.R. Tolkien is reported to have said that the word 'Celtic' had become "a magic bag, into which anything may be put, and out of which almost anything may come..."[15]

Sadly, this does appear to be the case; in many respects the current 'revival' of Celtic spirituality is more reinvention than rediscovery.[16] In order to avoid the pitfalls of anachronism, then, any study of the subject must use the earliest possible sources, seek to understand the period on its own terms, and keep everything in its proper historical context. I will endeavour to do all three.

[14] Donald E. Meek, "Surveying the Saints: Reflections on recent writings on 'Celtic Christianity'", *Scottish Bulletin of Evangelical Theology* 15, 1997, p 58
[15] J.R.R. Tolkien, *Angles and Britons,* (Cardiff: UWP, 1963), p 29f; cited in Ian Bradley, *Celtic Christianity: Making Myths and Chasing Dreams* (Edinburgh: EUP, 1999), p 226
[16] Sheldrake, *Living between Two Worlds* (London: DLT, 1995), p 94

1. A Survey of Early Celtic Sources

The following is not intended to be a comprehensive survey; rather it highlights the chief sources I have used in chapters 3 and 4, and gives some indication of their reliability.

The primary historical source for the period is the Venerable Bede's *Ecclesiastical History of the English people*, written for King Ceolwulf in five volumes and completed in 731AD. Bede (673-739 AD) was a monk living at Jarrow in Northumbria. He was not himself a Celt, and disagreed with them on a number of issues. Nonetheless, he belonged to a monastery of Celtic foundation and clearly approves of the Celts' love of scripture and their missionary zeal – to such an extent, indeed, that he may well be guilty of exaggeration. In the preface to his history, he acknowledges the importance of sources, freely admitting that his material is by no means all first hand, and that his first book especially is very dependent on an earlier preacher-historian called Gildas. Therefore the later volumes are generally considered to be more reliable than the first.

Most of the other primary source material centres on the Celtic Christians themselves, especially Patrick and Brigit in Ireland, Columba in Scotland, Cuthbert, Aidan and Hilda in Northumbria, Pelagius and Gildas in Wales, Columbanus in Gaul and Italy. Plus Brendan, Bueno, Cummean, Padarn, Ultán and a host of less well-known individuals.

Little of the material relating to them is directly theological. This is because, while the Roman church was busy convening councils and appealing to Church Fathers, many of the Celts whose writings survive and have become popular were less inclined toward theological debate. As a result, most of the evidence for their theology has to be derived from more devotional and practical material such as prayers, sermons and penitentials. For convenience, I have divided the literature into groups according to geographical provenance.

1.1.   Irish literature

This centres on the corpus of material linked to Patrick. Patrick was kidnapped from his home in Britain by pirates at the age of sixteen. At the time he was a nominal Christian. He was sold to an Irish farmer and endured six years of slavery before escaping back to Britain. During his slavery, he began to pray in earnest and was, as far as we can tell, soundly converted. He was later called by the Lord to return to Ireland as a missionary, and eventually became Bishop of his Irish flock.

Two of the earliest and most reliable works are those written by Patrick himself, namely Patrick's *Confession* (c. 470 AD) and his *Letter to the soldiers of Coroticus* (5th century). [7]

The former is a defence of his ministry and a testimony to his experiences of the Lord's grace. The latter reprimands a band of renegade Roman soldiers for kidnapping some newly baptised Irish Christians, and urges them to repent and release their captives.

Other Irish literature includes:

   a) St Patrick's *Breastplate* (8th century or later) The 'breastplate' or '*lorica*', was a particular style of prayer for protection, based on Ephesians 6:11-18. A number of modern hymns are based on it, but there is no evidence that Patrick himself had any part in its writing.

   b) *The Breastplate of Laidcenn* (probably pre-661 AD, because Laidcenn died in that year).

   c) Various other loricae (breastplate prayers) and poems of the 8th – 9th centuries.

   d) *Ultán's Hymn* (7th century) – Ultán was an Irish Bishop; his 'hymn' is a prayer to Brigit.

---

[7] These and many other early Celtic texts are readily accessible in Oliver Davies (Ed.), *Celtic Spirituality* (New Jersey: Paulist Press, 1999); many are also online at (eg) www.ccel.org and www.lamp.ac.uk/celtic

e) *The Antiphonary of Bangor* (a late 7th century hymnbook).

f) Various sermons or homilies, including *The Cambrai Homily* (7th – 8th century).

g) The *Canons* of the first Synod of St Patrick (possibly late 6th century).

h) *The Penitential of Cummean* (the fullest of the Celtic penitentials; Cummean was an Irish Bishop who died in 662 AD).

i) *The Stowe Missal* (pre-800).

j) A number of *'Lives'* of the saints, including two on Patrick (see below).

1.2. Welsh literature

Early Welsh literature centres on the works of the heretic Pelagius and the preacher-historian Gildas. The Pelagian corpus (4th – 5th century) consists of a large number of theological, exegetical and monastic texts. The works of Gildas (early 6th century) include his 'history': *On the Ruin and Conquest of Britain* (*De Excidio et Conquesto Britanniae*), his *Penitential,* which is one of the earliest, and various fragments of letters.

Other Welsh literature includes:

a) Various old Welsh poems and prayers.

b) *The Black Book of Carmarthen* – a 13th century anthology of earlier works, apparently both Christian and pre-Christian.

c) A number of *'Lives'* of the saints, including one on David (see below).

1.3. Scottish literature

This centres on the work of Columba, an Irish monk who travelled to Scotland and founded a monastery on Iona in 563 AD. He (probably) wrote:

The *Altus Prosator* (late 6th – early 7th century) – an acrostic poem in praise of Christ

Other Scottish literature includes:

The Life of Columba by Adomnán (7th century; see below)

1.4. Gallic literature

For our purposes, this centres on the corpus of material linked to Columbanus. Columbanus (c543 – 615 AD) was an Irish theologian and missionary who travelled from Ireland to found several monasteries on the continent of Europe, including that of Bobbio in Italy.

His surviving literature includes:

> *The Rule of Columbanus*
>
> *The Penitential of Columbanus*
>
> *The Letters of Columbanus*
>
> Thirteen *Sermons of Columbanus*

Other Gallic literature includes a number of *'Lives'* including *The Life of Columbanus* by Jonas (see below)

A note on the *Lives* of the Saints (the *Vitae Sancti*):

Most of the *Lives* were written by monks for the purpose of clarifying what an exemplary Christian life looks like. Many, especially of the later ones, were also written with a view to promoting pilgrim visits to the shrine of their own monastery's particular saint. As a result, strict historical accuracy was not necessarily the author's primary concern. The majority date from the tenth to twelfth centuries, but the following are among the earlier ones:

a) *The Life of Samson* (possibly the earliest Life; 7th century)

b) *The Life of Patrick by Muirchú* (7th century)

c) *The Life of Columba by Adomnán* (7th century)

d) *The Life of Columbanus by Jonas* (7th century)

e) *The Life of St Brigit the Virgin by Cogitosus* (late 7th century)

f) *The Life of Cuthbert by Bede* (721AD)

By no means all early Celtic sources are in book form; there is also much artwork and imagery, for example on the stone high crosses which were often used as boundary markers, or in the form of illustrated manuscripts such as the Book of Kells (date uncertain) or the Lindisfarne Gospels (c. 700 AD, and available to view in the British Library).

2.   A Brief History of Early Celtic Christianity

No one knows when the Christian faith first came to Britain except that it must have been sometime during the first two centuries AD, presumably with the Romans. The sixth century abbot Gildas records that Britain received the "beams of light" of the gospel as early as the reign of Tiberius (pre- 37 AD), but Gildas may not be reliable.

However, both Tertullian (c.160-220 AD) and Origen (c.185-254 AD) mention British Christians and certainly, by the beginning of the fourth century, there was a church in Britain sufficiently established to send three bishops to the Council of Arles (314 AD). St. Alban was martyred in the late third or early fourth century. And a few years later this fledgling church even managed to produce its very own heretic (Pelagius c.360-420 AD).

However, with the Empire under attack, the Romans withdrew in 409-410 AD. The fiercely pagan Angles and Saxons took advantage of the opportunity to invade (from 449 onwards) and the Christian church was rapidly driven back to the extremities of northern Scotland, Wales, Cornwall and Ireland. In 397 AD Ninian founded the 'Candida Casa' (white house) monastery at Whithorn on the Solway Firth and used it as a missionary base from which to evangelise the far north.

The Celtic Christian era, however, is usually reckoned to date from Patrick's mission to Ireland in 431 AD. Columba was one of many who followed Patrick's example, founding several churches and monasteries in Ireland before leaving for Scotland in about 565 AD. There he founded the enormously influential monastery of Iona, from which missionaries went all over northern Britain, evangelising the pagans and founding further monastic centres. Aidan, for example, founded a monastery on Lindisfarne in Northumbria (635 AD), which was to become a major ecclesiastical centre. Hilda founded a double monastery (monks and nuns) at Whitby. And so on; by no means were all Celtic Christians monastic, but between the fifth and eighth centuries, hundreds of monasteries were founded.

Solitary monks did exist, but most lived in communities. In the early Celtic centuries, these communities were inclusive of men and women, married and celibate, clergy and lay, slave and free. Some were single sex; others were 'double' monasteries. And abbots could be male, or female like Hilda at Whitby or Brigit at Kildare in Ireland. Over the years, the monasteries grew in both political and economic importance. Eventually they provided most, though not all, of the Celtic churches' bishops. The Celtic churches were not organised into dioceses on the Roman system, so abbots generally had great freedom and authority. Their monasteries became influential centres of Celtic society.

Rome began to assert its supremacy again in the latter part of the sixth century. Pope Gregory, troubled by the dominance of the pagan Anglo-Saxons, commissioned Augustine and forty others as missionaries to Britain in 597 AD. Progress was slow, but inevitably Augustine's presence highlighted the differences between the Roman church and the Celtic churches. Augustine himself died in 604 AD, but it was another sixty years before the differences were finally resolved at the Synod of Whitby in 664 AD. There, the Celtic bishop Colman discussed with the Roman bishop Wilfrid such knotty issues as the style of monks' tonsures, the date of Easter and the number of bishops required to consecrate a new bishop. Wilfrid won, and from that time on, Celtic Christianity declined in England, Wales and Scotland. Iona finally celebrated Easter the Roman way in 716 AD. In Ireland, most of the church had adopted Roman practice by the end of the eighth century. Monastic life became increasingly lax, provoking the Célí Dé reforms from the eighth century onwards. The 1152 Synod of Kells, which organised the church into Roman dioceses, marks an official end to the Celtic period in Ireland, although many would associate the endpoint with the arrival of the Normans in 1169.

3. Distinctive Features of Early Celtic Theology

Discovering Celtic theology is not an easy task. Not only are reliable primary theological texts rare but, as already indicated, although they aimed to be biblically orthodox, many Celtic Christians whose writings are now popular were not primarily interested in wrestling with theological doctrines.[18] As Columbanus famously maintained, the Christian life is better lived than debated.[19] However, spirituality is dependent on theology. Therefore it is not a fruitless exercise to explore Celtic prayers, sermons, testimonies, letters, monastic Rules and penitentials in the search for Celtic theology. For convenience I have (somewhat arbitrarily) organised the results along broadly systematic lines.

3.1. God

The Celtic Christians managed to maintain a healthy balance between God's transcendence and his immanence, possibly because they were less influenced by neoplatonist thinking than were the Roman churches.

With regard to transcendence, their prayers reveal belief in a God who was 'above and beyond' all time and all creation. Their God was the Almighty Lord; always deserving of praise, in control of all circumstances; with the power to change circumstances, and especially with the power to save sinners from judgement and hell.

---

[18] O'Loughlin demonstrates that some of the Irish clergy were interested in theological debate. See O'Loughlin, T. *Celtic Theology: Humanity, World and God in Early Irish Writings* (London: Continuum, 2000).
However, these works rarely feature large, either in anthologies of early material or in contemporary 'Celtic' literature.

[19] Columbanus, *Instructiones* (Sermons) 1:5 in *Sancti Columbani Opera* (ed. Walker, G.S.M., Dublin, 1970).

> Almighty Creator, it is you who made the land and the sea...
> He who made the wonder of the world will save us, has saved us.
> It is not too great a toil to praise the Trinity.
> Clear and high in the perfect assembly,
> Let us praise above the nine orders of angels
> The sublime and blessed Trinity...
> The one who has both wisdom and dominion
> above heaven, below heaven, completely...[20]

This lovely early Welsh praise poem demonstrates not only that original Celtic Christianity was thoroughly theocentric, but also that it was thoroughly Trinitarian, a characteristic which may be observed in that most well known of all Celtic prayers, 'Patrick's Breastplate':

> I rise today through a mighty power, calling upon the Holy Trinity,
> affirming the threeness, confessing the oneness, of Creation's Creator.[21]

Indeed, the Trinity was such a strong feature of Celtic prayer that Esther de Waal devotes a whole chapter of her book to it, citing many examples, some of which reveal a clear belief in the distinctive roles of the three persons of the Trinity.

> O Father who wrought me, O Son who bought me, O Spirit who sought me, Let me be Thine.[22]

Which brings us back to the fact that, for the Celts, God the Holy Trinity was both transcendent and immanent.

With regard to immanence, their prayers reveal belief in a God who is always present, all-seeing and all-caring. Further still, and much more significantly, many of these prayers leave the reader in no

---

[20]   from an early Welsh praise poem, in Davies, *Celtic Spirituality*, p 266
[21]   from *Patrick's Breastplate*, in a synthesis of different translations.
[22]   An Irish blessing, in Douglas Hyde *Religious Songs of Connacht II* (originally pub 1906; rep. Shannon: IUP, 1972), p 369

doubt about the existence of an intimate personal relationship between the Christian and the Lord God.

> O God, Lord of creation... You are my king. You are my law. Yours is my flesh, my body. I love you, blessed Christ, for my soul is yours tonight. Let me not conceal it, O King. May I be in your royal dwelling all my days...[23]

The same is true of longer prose works such as Patrick's *Confession*, which contains clear evidence of genuine conversion and a growing love for Christ:

> The Lord... made me aware of my unbelief that I might at last advert to my sins and turn whole-heartedly to the Lord my God. He showed concern for my weakness, and pity for my youth and ignorance; he watched over me before I got to know him and before I was wise or distinguished good from evil. In fact, he protected me and comforted me as a father would his son. I cannot be silent then, nor indeed should I, about the great benefits and grace that the Lord saw fit to confer on me...... From the time in my early manhood when I came to know him, the love of God and reverence for him have grown in me, and up to now, by the favour of God, I have kept the faith.[24]

Without succumbing to any irreverence, these Celtic Christians behaved toward the Lord as children confident of their heavenly Father's loving concern for them. They regarded him as ever approachable and willing to hear and answer their prayers, no matter how small or ordinary.

Inevitably, then, the incarnation was important to them, for Christ was God revealed – living and powerful, the conqueror of death and the giver of life. Celtic Christianity was strongly

---

[23] from an 8th – 9th century prayer book, in Davies, *Celtic Spirituality*, p 289
[24] Patrick's *Confession*, paras 2, 44; translation by Joseph Duffy in *Patrick in his own Words* (Dublin: Veritas, 2000)

Christocentric; so much so that in some of their devotional writings, Jesus Christ seems to be an almost tangible companion through life.

> Christ with me, Christ before me, Christ behind me;
> Christ within me, Christ beneath me, Christ above me;
> Christ to right of me, Christ to left of me;
> Christ in my lying, Christ in my sitting, Christ in my rising;
> Christ in the heart of all who think of me,
> Christ on the tongue of all who speak to me,
> Christ in the eye of all who see me,
> Christ in the ear of all who hear me.[25]

> O holy Jesus, gentle friend, morning star, midday sun adorned,
> Brilliant flame of righteousness, life everlasting and eternity,
> Fountain ever new, ever-living, ever-lasting,
> Heart's desire of patriarchs, longing of prophets, master of apostles and disciples,
> Giver of the law, Prince of the New Testament, Judge of doom,
> Son of the merciful Father without mother in heaven,
> Son of the true virgin Mary, without father on earth,
> True and loving brother,
> For the sake of your affection, hear the entreaty of this mean wretch...[26]

The help of the Holy Spirit too was frequently sought in the pursuit of holiness.

> Shame on my thoughts, how they stray from me!....
> O beloved, truly chaste Christ, to whom every eye is clear,
> May the grace of the sevenfold Spirit come to keep them, to hold them in check.[27]

On a more explicitly theological level, Patrick's *Confession* neatly summarises early Celtic theology concerning God. (Reflecting as it does

---

[25] from *Patrick's Breastplate*, in Davies, *Celtic Spirituality*, p 120
[26] from *the Broom of Devotion*, in Davies, *Celtic Spirituality*, p 295
[27] from an early Irish prayer, in Davies, *Celtic Spirituality*, p 262

so the Nicean and other Christological controversies which plagued the 4th century church.) Paragraph 4 of his 'Confession' for example:

> For there is no other God, nor ever was before, nor shall be hereafter, but God the Father, unbegotten and without beginning, in whom all things began, whose are all things, as we have been taught; and his son Jesus Christ, who manifestly always existed with the Father, before the beginning of time in the spirit with the Father, indescribably begotten before all things, and all things visible and invisible were made by him. He was made man, conquered death and was received into heaven, to the Father who gave him all power over every name in heaven and on earth and in hell, so that every tongue should confess that Jesus Christ is Lord and God, in whom we believe. And we look to his imminent coming again, the judge of the living and the dead, who will render to each according to his deeds. And he poured out his Holy Spirit on us in abundance, the gift and pledge of immortality, which makes those who believe and listen into sons of God and co-heirs of Christ who is revealed, and we worship one God in the Trinity of the holy name.[28]

3.2. Creation

For Celtic Christians, one of the implications of belief in God as the Almighty Creator was that creation itself should be reverenced and enjoyed. For ascetic monks living in wild and isolated places, this was not difficult. Sea and wind, fire and snow, birds, flowers, cows: anything good or beautiful in the Lord's creation was taken to reflect the goodness and beauty of the Lord himself. As a result there exists a whole body of 'nature poetry' – prayers and verses which reflect a poetic appreciation and thankfulness for different elements of the natural world.

A hedge of trees surrounds me, a blackbird's lay sings to me,

---

[28] Patrick's *Confession*, para 4, in a synthesis of different translations.

> Praise I shall not conceal.
> Above my lined book the trilling of the birds sings to me.
> A clear-voiced cuckoo sings to me in a gray cloak from the tops of the bushes,
> May the Lord save me from judgement; well do I write under the greenwood.[29]

And creation was frequently called upon to join in the praise of the Lord, especially in the words of the *Benedicite*, the canticle most commonly sung in Celtic monasteries.

However, in spite of a very positive view of creation, the early Celts did not make the mistake of confusing creation with its Creator. God was still transcendent, not trapped within his creation, nor limited in any way by it. And although creation could and did reveal something of the Lord, it could never reveal him fully.

> The world cannot comprehend in song bright and melodious,
> Even though the grass and trees should sing,
> All your wonders, O true Lord! [30]

Nor could it reveal him with absolute reliability, for the Celts recognised also that creation was fallen, transient, corrupt, and needing redemption.

> Pay no heed, pay no heed to the world and its way,
> Give no love, give no love to what lasts but a day.
> Have no care, have no care for the meaningless earth.
> Lay no hold, lay no hold on its gaiety and mirth...
> The world is running out like the ebbing sea:
> Fly far from it and seek safety. [31]

---

[29] An early Irish poem, in Davies, *Celtic Spirituality*, p 259
[30] from a 9th century Welsh poem, *Juvencus Englynion*, cited in A.M. Allchin, "There is no Resurrection where there is no Earth" in Atherton (ed.) *Celts and Christians*, p 106
[31] Bamford and Marsh, *Celtic Christianity: Ecology and Holiness* (Edinburgh: Floris, 1986), p 83

3.3. Sin and salvation

Of course it was understood that the Fall affected people too; indeed the sinfulness of human nature featured very large in Celtic Christianity. Many of their writings incorporate an element of confession for sin, and there exist a number of 'penitentials' detailing specific penances for specific sins. Patrick's *Confession*, for example, begins: "I am Patrick, I am a sinner: the most unsophisticated of people; the least among all the Christians..."[32] and throughout his writings, he frequently mentions the realities of judgement and hell.

Likewise Columba wrote:

> It appears that no one doubts that hell is in the lowest regions, where darkness, worms and dreadful beasts are held; where sulphurous fire burns with consuming flames, where men's faces are contorted, and there is 'weeping and gnashing of teeth'...

> 'The Day of the Lord, the King of Kings, is near.' 'The Day of Wrath,' 'of vengeance,' of darkness and clouds; the day of thunders, mighty and wonderful; the day of affliction, mourning and sadness...

> Before the Lord's tribunal we shall stand shivering with fear. We shall offer an explanation for all our undertakings, while we see our crimes placed before our sight, with the books of conscience laid open in front of us. Then we shall break into the most bitter crying and gasping; for the possibility of doing something about [our sins] will have been taken away. [33]

Sin and coming judgement were serious matters. So much so that Patrick found an unnamed but fully confessed sin, committed when he was fifteen, still caused him great difficulty years later, when British elders cited it as a reason for opposing his mission to Ireland.

---

[32] Patrick's *Confession*, para 1, in Davies, *Celtic Spirituality*, p 67
[33] from Columba's *Altus Prosator*, in Davies, *Celtic Spirituality*, p 408f

Perhaps it is not surprising that so many early Celtic prayers are prayers for freedom from every sin and for salvation from 'the fire of hell and judgement'.

> I beseech you... that you will take me under your protection, defense, and care, to preserve and protect me from devils and all their promptings against all the elements of the world, against lusts, against transgressions, against sins, against worldly crimes, against the dangers of this life and the torments of the next, from the hands of enemies and every terror, against the fire of hell and judgement, against shame before the face of God, against the attacks of devils, that they may have no power over us at our entry into the next world...[34]

Fortunately it wasn't only sin, judgement and hell which featured large in Celtic Christianity, for Jesus Christ was alive and reigning at the Father's right hand. His cross, resurrection and ascension featured equally large, and the power of the Holy Spirit was ever available to be called upon.

> Shame on my thoughts, how they stray from me!
> I fear great danger from this on the Day of eternal Judgement.
> During the Psalms they wander on a path that is not right:
> They run, they distract, they misbehave before the eyes of the great God...
> O beloved, truly chaste Christ, to whom every eye is clear,
> May the grace of the sevenfold Spirit come to keep them, to hold them in check!
> Rule this heart of mine, O swift God of the elements,
> that you may be my love, and that I may do your will![35]

As they freely admitted their sins so they also emphasised their need for the forgiveness and new life which could only be found 'in Christ', and especially through his blood shed on the cross.

---

[34] from the *Broom of Devotion*, in Davies, *Celtic Spirituality*, p 295
[35] from an early Irish prayer in Davies, *Celtic Spirituality*, p 262

Giver of salvation, Christ the Son of God,
Has saved the world by his cross and blood.
The Lord has been sacrificed for all,
Himself both priest and victim. [36]

The cross and resurrection of Christ feature prominently in Celtic imagery, especially in the form of the many stone 'high crosses' still to be found throughout Ireland. However, the most common reference to the cross is in the context of those early prayers for protection known as 'Breastplate prayers' or 'loricae', of which St Patrick's is the most famous example:

I rise today
in the power of Christ's birth and baptism,
in the power of his crucifixion and burial,
in the power of his rising and ascending,
in the power of his descending and judging...[37]

Salvation was to be found only in Christ. So Patrick's *Breastplate* ends with the words:

For to the Lord belongs salvation,
and to the Lord belongs salvation
and to Christ belongs salvation.
May your salvation, Lord, be with us always. [38]

And Columba's *Altus Prosator* continues:

The banner of the cross, the brightest sign, will shine resplendent,
When Christ, the celestial Lord, descends from the heavens...
Then the Trinity will be praised;
With the singing of hymns rung out with prayer...
The furious zeal of the fire will consume the adversaries,
Those who will not have faith that Christ came from God

---

[36]   from an Irish communion hymn in Davies, *Celtic Spirituality*, p 316
[37]   from *Patrick's Breastplate*, in Davies, *Celtic Spirituality*, p 118
[38]   Ibid., p 120

the Father.
But we, by contrast, shall fly at once to meet him,
And so shall be with him in the various ordered ranks,
According to the eternal rewards we deserve,
Remaining in glory forever and ever. [39]

The *Altus Prosator* is only one of many writings which make it clear that good works did matter to the Christian Celts. And undoubtedly some individuals did thereby fall into the trap of treating them as salvific. It is, indeed, hard to read some texts, especially some of the later ones, *without* seeing 'salvation by works'. Consider the following extract from an Irish sermon, for example:

> It is into hell that God shall cast sinners on Judgment Day... hell with its many and great torments... In this way, then, these punishments are to be avoided: by hard work and study, by fasting and prayer, by righteousness and mercy, by faith and love...We should strive then for the kingdom of heaven... May we enter the kingdom of that King, may we merit it and may we dwell there forever and ever, Amen. [40]

The earlier texts, however, are generally much more biblically orthodox. Patrick's *Confession*, in particular, repeatedly quotes from the book of Romans as he attributes his conversion, his spiritual growth and his ministry all to the Lord's 'great grace.' The only reason good works (in his case chiefly of evangelism) do still matter is because the Lord has graciously saved him.

> It would be neither right nor proper for me to do anything but to tell you of all the many blessings and great grace which the Lord saw fit to give me... He gave me a great grace...It was not my grace, but God who conquered in me... Truly I am greatly in God's debt... So it is right and proper that we should fish well and carefully...Therefore, 'I shall give to him for all the things that he has given to me.' But what shall I say to him?

---

[39] from Columba's *Altus Prosator*, in Davies, *Celtic Spirituality*, p 410
[40] from a 9th century Old Irish homily, in Davies, *Celtic Spirituality*, p 366ff

> What can I promise to give my Lord? I have nothing of value that is not his gift! [41]

In other words, it seems that the charge of Pelagianism which is sometimes levelled against the whole of Celtic Christianity[42] is unwarranted, at least as a general characteristic. Pelagius Britto was indeed himself ethnically a Celt (dates uncertain, but about 360-420 AD). He was a lay monk, deeply ascetic, and commendably troubled by the lukewarm nature of much of the 'Christianity' of his day. Like most Celts, he had a high view of creation and took sin very seriously. But Pelagius had *such* a high view of creation that he rejected the doctrine of original sin and taught that humans had the ability both to choose and to do good rather than evil. Therefore it was incumbent upon them to seek to achieve, by good works, that holiness which was necessary for salvation. Thus the 'gospel' of Pelagius denied the internal operation of sanctifying grace and, in practice, had more in common with stoicism than biblical Christianity. Inevitably, then, Pelagius found himself in conflict with Augustine (of Hippo), who rigorously defended biblical orthodoxy. Pelagianism was denounced as heretical by the Council of Carthage in 418 AD, but lingered on, especially in some parts of Britain and Gaul, until the second synod of Orange in 529 AD.

Those who believe that the majority of Celtic churches were strongly influenced by Pelagius often argue that these churches were isolated communities, forced to the extremities of Britain and Ireland by the invasion of pagan Angles and Saxons, and so largely untouched by Roman views and Roman authority. Certainly it is true that Patrick thought Ireland constituted the "outermost regions beyond which no one lives."[43] Certainly, Bede testifies to Pelagianism as a recurring problem among the Celts, albeit apparently a minority

---

[41] Patrick's *Confession*, paras 3, 5, 37, 38, 57, in Davies, *Celtic Spirituality*, pp 67-83
[42] by, eg. Van de Weyer, Hull, Mackey and O'Donoghue (see Bibliography), each with different emphases.
[43] Patrick's *Confession*, para 34, in Davies, *Celtic Spirituality*, p 76

one.[44] Certainly Celtic monasteries were relatively independent, each having its own 'Rule' (four of which survive from before 800AD). Certainly there were a number of areas in which Celtic practice differed from Roman practice, such as the dating of Easter, and the style of monks' tonsures.[45] Certainly Columbanus, though he dealt respectfully with Pope Gregory I, refused to submit to his authority on certain issues.[46]

But such arguments can easily become anachronistic. This was the period before the Benedictine Rule became the official norm, when there was a wide diversity of practice throughout the monasteries of Western Europe. And Márkus and others have effectively argued that, in fact, Irish Christians never considered themselves beyond the remit of Roman authority.[47]

Furthermore, Pelagius spent most of his adult life either in Rome or in various countries around the Mediterranean. Therefore the extent to which he influenced, or was influenced by, Celtic distinctives is highly debatable.

And, although he never directly addresses the Pelagian debate, Patrick's theology in the *Confession* is clearly Augustinian. The quote below, for example, clearly reflects his firm belief in both his own inability to do good of himself and the internal operation of divine grace.

> It was not my grace, but God who conquered in me... as long as I am in this body of death I do not trust myself because he is strong who daily tries to drag me away from faith... the hostile flesh is always drawing me toward death, namely toward doing those enticing things which are forbidden... Then I was not quick to acknowledge the grace that was in

---

[44] Bede, *Ecclesiastical History of the English People*, London: Penguin, 1955, Book I:17, 21; Book II:19

[45] For further details, see chapter 2

[46] this is evident in his letter to Gregory re the date of Easter, *Epistola* CXXVII, online at www.ccel.org

[47] Márkus, "The End of Celtic Christianity", in *Epworth Review* 24, 1997, pp 45-55.

me; now what I ought to have done before seems right to me.[48]

So it seems that Patrick, at least, had grasped the very heart of genuine Christianity, and that early Celtic theology was generally biblically orthodox. How then did the Celts practice their faith?

4. Distinctive Features of Early Celtic Spirituality

The Celts may not have been great theologians, but they were great pray-ers. They prayed over great matters and small ones; they prayed in crisis and they prayed through every detail of ordinary life, from waking in the morning to going to bed, as well as for births, deaths, and other more major life events. For example:

> The first word I say in the morning, when I arise:
> May Christ's cross be my armour about me... [49]
> May your holy angels, O Christ, Son of the living God,
> tend our sleep, our rest, our bright bed...
> May our waking, our work, and our living be holy;
> Our sleep, our rest, without hindrance or harm. [50]

For Celtic Christians there was no false dichotomy between the sacred and the secular; the whole of life was to be bathed in prayer. The implication is that the Lord sees every detail and cares about every detail. So it's hardly surprising to discover that this 'praying over all areas of life' was accompanied by the pursuit of holiness in all areas of life. This was exemplified particularly in the monasteries, where the pursuit of holiness meant obedience first to the Word and then to the Rule.

The Word was central to Celtic monastic life. Not only did the monks carefully copy and illustrate the scriptures, producing beautiful manuscripts such as the Lindisfarne Gospels and the Book of Kells, but they would also study the Bible (using the few available commentaries), memorise long passages, and quote it frequently in their writings. In Patrick's two surviving works for example, there are some 340 quotations from 46 biblical books,[51] albeit mostly of the

---

[49] from a Welsh poem, in Davies, *Celtic Spirituality*, p 274
[50] from a prayer in Davies, *Celtic Spirituality*, p 289
[51] according to Mitton, *Restoring the Woven Cord*, p 26

'proof-text' variety. (Like their 'heroes' the Desert Fathers, Celtic interpretation of scripture tended to be either very literal or very allegorical; little attention was paid to context, genre etc.) The $7^{th} - 8^{th}$ Century monk historian Bede testifies to the fact that what they read they also lived. Although he disagreed with Celtic Christians on a number of issues, nonetheless he commends the monks of Iona because they "diligently followed whatever pure and devout customs they learned in the prophets, the Gospels, and the writings of the Apostles."[52] Nor were the scriptures necessarily confined to the monasteries. In Ireland, for example, the production of small 'pocket gospels' suggests they were used while travelling, or by people who could not afford whole Bibles.

The Rule described the character and pattern of a monk's daily life. Its overall challenge was to biblical discipleship; the practical details of life in a specific monastic community were always secondary. So, for example, Columbanus' *Rule for Monks* begins: "First of all we are taught to love God with all our heart, all our mind, and all our strength, and our neighbours as ourselves; and then our works." Then follows a call to obey the abbot (even to death, in imitation of Christ's obedience) and to forego the comforts of life in favour of silence, poverty, chastity, humility and mortification.[53]

In other words, the *Rule* of Columbanus, like the other three surviving Celtic Rules, promoted a life of severe asceticism. It seems these Celtic Christians were consciously trying to imitate not only Christ himself but their other 'heroes of faith', the 3rd Century 'Desert Fathers'. Several texts name two in particular: Anthony of Egypt and Paul of Thebes.

> I praise two, Who is one and two, Who is truly three,...
> God is his name... the God of Paul and Anthony. [54]

---

[52] Bede, *Ecclesiastical History of the English People*, Book III:4, p 149
[53] from *The Rule for Monks* by Columbanus, in Davies, *Celtic Spirituality*, pp 246-256
[54] from an early Welsh poem, in Davies, *Celtic Spirituality*, p 268

Emulating Paul and Anthony involved building monasteries in inhospitable, inaccessible places such as Iona, Lindisfarne or Skelling Michael (a rock in the Atlantic)[55]. It might prompt monks to pray for long periods while standing in icy water, or with arms outstretched.[56] It might prompt them retreat from community life into solitary study and prayer; it might prompt them to to eat only bread with a few vegetables, or to fast altogether for many days. For example, Bede records that Adomnán ate food only on Sundays and Thursdays[57], and one anonymous Irish monk wrote the following poem:

> All alone in my little cell, without the company of anyone;
> precious has been the pilgrimage before going to meet death...
> Sanctifying the body by good habits, trampling like a man upon it;
> With weak and tearful eyes for the forgiveness of my passions...
> My food as befits my station, precious has been the captivity:
> My dinner, without doubt, would not make me full-blooded.
> Dry bread weighed out, well we bow the head;
> Water of the many coloured hillside, that is the drink I would take.
> A bitter, meagre dinner; diligently feeding the sick;
> Keeping off strife and visits; a calm serene conscience.
> It would be desirable, a pure and holy blemish:
> Cheeks withered and sunken, a shrivelled, leathery skin.
> Treading the paths of the gospel; singing Psalms at every hour;
> An end of talking and long stories; constant bending of the knees... [58]

---

[55] It is still possible to see the Celtic monks' beehive shaped cells on Skellig Michael.

[56] Aidan, Cuthbert and a monk called Drythelm are all known to have prayed like this.

[57] Bede, *Ecclesiastical History of the English People*, Book IV:25, p 252

[58] from an Irish poem in Davies, *Celtic Spirituality*, p 260; ostensibly the work of a 7th century anchorite, but possibly that of a 9th century monk imagining the life of a 7th century anchorite, in which case the asceticism may be idealized. It is nonetheless unlikely to be entirely fictitious.

Columbanus justified such asceticism on the grounds that "the possibility of spiritual progress may be kept alive by an abstinence which punishes the flesh."[59]

As a further aid to the 'possibility of spiritual progress', penances also featured large in Celtic monastic life. Monks who erred, and especially priests, were subject to the harshest penances lasting from a few days to several years. *The Penitential of Cummean*, for example, prescribes beatings for monks in addition to fastings and/or saying a specified number of penitential psalms. For children and laypeople, penances were less severe, but still involved going without meals or eating only bread and water.

All these penances are described as "medicine for the salvation of souls" and "remedies for wounds"[60]. They were an indication of the seriousness with which post-baptismal sin was regarded. According to one early Irish text, they were also part of a threefold remedy for such sin, consisting of "a pool of tears of repentance, a pool wrung out of blood in penance, a pool of sweat in labour."[61] They worked on the principle that "they who do what is forbidden without restraint ought to restrain themselves even from what is allowed,"[62] (a principle known as 'curing by contraries.')

The *Penitential of Cummean* details penances for eight "principal vices", namely gluttony, fornication, avarice, anger, depression, apathy, vanity and pride, along with various "minor cases" and errors to be avoided in "guarding the host". It makes clear, however, that there must remain room for flexibility in assigning them, saying:

> this is to be carefully observed in all penance: the length of time anyone remains in his faults, what education he has

---

[59] from *The Rule for Monks* by Columbanus, para 3 in Davies, *Celtic Spirituality*, p 248

[60] *The Penitential of Cummean*, in Davies, *Celtic Spirituality*, p 230

[61] translation of *Apgitir Chrabaid* from T.O. Clancy and G. Márkus (eds) *Iona: The Earliest Poetry of a Celtic Monastery*, Edinburgh, 1995, p.205f cited in Allchin, "There is no Resurrection where there is no Earth", in Atherton (ed.) *Celts and Christians*, p 116

[62] *The Penitential of Cummean*, in Davies, *Celtic Spirituality*, p 231

received, with what passion he is assailed, with what courage
he resists, with what intensity of weeping he seems to be
afflicted, with what pressure he is driven to sin.[63]

For Celtic Christians, the practice of penance usually involved the
help of a 'soul friend' or 'anamchara', again a concept inherited from
the Desert Fathers. 'Soul friends' could be of any ecclesiastical status
(not necessarily priests), though they were usually older, more
experienced Christians. Their overriding concern was to do whatever
they could to promote the spiritual growth of their charges until they
reached that maturity in Christ which is Christlikeness. They were
people with whom Christians could share, discuss, and pray about
every detail of their spiritual lives – the joys and sadnesses, spiritual
encouragements and spiritual battles, including confession and
penance as appropriate.

For a Celtic monk, one of the topics of conversation and
prayer with one's anamchara would be pilgrimage, and pilgrimage of
a peculiarly Celtic kind. Not so much journeying to a site of special
Christian significance, but leaving home to wander as an 'alien and
exile'[64] in this world, often with no specific destination in mind, but
with a decidedly missionary outcome.[65] The Anglo-Saxon Chronicle
records an instance of this practice in the annal for 891:

> Three Scots in a boat without any oars came to King Alfred
> from Ireland, which they left because they wanted, for the
> love of God, to be on pilgrimage, and they did not care
> where.[66]

Such pilgrims were called 'peregrinati' and the result of their
'wanderings' was the conversion of thousands who were previously
pagan and the foundation of many new monasteries.

---

[63] *The Penitential of Cummean*, in Davies, *Celtic Spirituality*, p 245
[64] see 1 Peter 2:11
[65] Whether or not mission was always the primary purpose of their pilgrimages is
debatable, but, at the very least, it was a remarkable side-effect of several
pilgrimages.
[66] cited by Atherton, in *Celts and Christians*, p 10

So, for example, Columba, after founding several monasteries in Ireland, travelled in about 565 AD to the land of the Picts where, according to Bede, he "converted that people to the faith of Christ by his preaching and example"[67], then founded the influential monastery of Iona. From Iona, peregrinati travelled all over northern Britain, preaching the gospel as they went. They evangelised a vast area, and their influence spread as far south as the Thames. Among them was Aidan, whose pilgrimage led him East, to preach among the Northumbrians and found the monastery of Lindisfarne (635 AD). Bede records that he:

> always travelled on foot unless compelled by necessity to ride; and whatever people he met on his walks, whether high or low, he stopped and spoke to them. If they were heathen, he urged them to be baptised; and if they were Christians, he strengthened their faith...[68]

Similarly, David of Wales founded twelve monasteries in Somerset, Lincoln, Derby, Hereford and Wales. Columbanus founded three monasteries in Burgundy before moving on to found another at Bobbio in Italy, and so on. Ian Bradley has gone so far as to claim that pilgrimage is the "single most important and distinctive theme" of Celtic spirituality.[69] He may overstate the case, especially as this form of pilgrimage seems to have become gradually less popular from the ninth century onwards.

Nevertheless, to the extent that it is true, it is probably because pilgrimage was linked in the Celtic mind with the desire for martyrdom. Celtic Christians took their faith so seriously that they were more than ready to suffer for Christ's sake, even to death. Consider, for example, Patrick's testimony:

> What return can I make to him for all his goodness to me?... I

---

[67] Bede, *Ecclesiastical History of the English People*, Book III:4, p 148
[68] Bede, *Ecclesiastical History of the English People*, Book III:5, p 150
[69] Ian Bradley, *Colonies of Heaven: Celtic Models for Today's Church* (London: DLT, 2000), p 197

am ready and indeed greatly desire it that he should give me
his cup to drink, as he gave it to others who loved him...
I beg of him the grace to shed my blood...[70]

But it was not given to everyone to die for Christ, so Celts held that
there were other forms of martyrdom. Each was associated with a
different colour. To suffer death for Christ was red martyrdom, which
was undoubtedly the kind most desired. Then white martyrdom was
to renounce the world in order to suffer the privations of life as a
monk or hermit. And the sufferings entailed in the struggle for
mastery of one's desires through penances was known as 'green
martyrdom' (or, in some translations, blue).[71] This last seems to have
been peculiarly Irish, and one expression of it would be to leave home
and go on missionary pilgrimage for Christ's sake.

However, the evangelistic missionary activity which was
central to Celtic Christianity was not simply rooted in monastic
penance. Its foundations were solidly biblical. Patrick considered
himself "bound by the Spirit... a servant in Christ to a far-off nation
on account of the indescribable glory of eternal life which is in Christ
Jesus our Lord."[72]

Therefore, as he explains,

It is right and proper that we should fish well and carefully –
as the Lord warns and teaches us saying, 'Come after me and
I shall make you fishers of men.' And again he says through
the prophets, 'Behold I send out fishermen and any hunters,
says God', and so forth. So truly it is our task to cast our nets
and catch 'a great multitude' and crowd for God...[73]

And he goes on to quote Matthew 28:19f, John 19:37, Matthew 24:14,
Acts 2:17f and Romans 9:25f in support.

---

[70] Patrick's *Confession*, paras 57,59, in Duffy, *Patrick in his own Words*, p 27
[71] These three martyrdoms are detailed in *The Cambrai Homily*, in Davies, *Celtic Spirituality*, p 370
[72] Patrick, *A Letter to the Soldiers of Coroticus*, para 10 in Davies, *Celtic Spirituality*, p 86
[73] Patrick's *Confession*, para 40, in Davies, *Celtic Spirituality*, p 77

Not that evangelism was the sole element of mission. Celtic Churches and monasteries were also caring and generous towards the poor, and hospitable to allcomers. Their frugal simplicity of life attracted ordinary people, and many of them actively sought to relieve oppression and ensure justice. For example, when a renegade Roman soldier called Coroticus kidnapped some Irish Christians to sell into slavery, Patrick wrote a stinging letter pleading for their release.[74]

Christian Celts like Patrick understood that such 'fishing', whatever form it took, would entail hard spiritual warfare on a number of fronts. Most immediately, it entailed confrontation with sun-worshipping pagans, and especially their druids. There is no doubt Patrick firmly believed that "all those miserable people who worship [the sun] shall end up in a foul punishment."[75] Nevertheless, the Christians' approach was twofold. They would directly denounce and oppose such practices as animal, or even human, sacrifice, and there are many tales of Patrick, Columba and others courageously doing just that at considerable cost. Patrick testifies to suffering "many persecutions even including chains"[76] for the gospel. But at the same time, they would try to accommodate more 'neutral' elements of the pagan culture by 'Christianising' them post-conversion. So, for example, the originally pagan 'Breastplate' style of prayer was preserved; wells which had been dedicated to pagan idols (eg. the water sprite 'Eilan') were subsequently dedicated to similar-sounding saints ('Helen');[77] St Brigid's day was timed to coincide with the pagan festival of Imbolc, and so on.[78] And although, like Patrick, Columba had no doubt that

The furious zeal of the fire will consume the adversaries,

---

[74] Patrick, *A Letter to the Soldiers of Coroticus*, in Davies, *Celtic Spirituality*, pp 84-89

[75] Patrick's *Confession* para 60, in Davies, *Celtic Spirituality*, p 82

[76] Patrick's *Confession*, para 37, in Davies, *Celtic Spirituality*, p 76

[77] an example cited in Mitton, *Restoring the Woven Cord*, p 91f

[78] Some claim Brigid herself was no more than a 'Christianised' pagan goddess, but there is no direct evidence for the claim, and it seems most unlikely given the general orthodoxy of the early Irish Christians.

Those who will not have faith that Christ came from God the
Father,"[79]

yet he is famously reputed to have spoken these words:

"My Druid is Christ, the Son of God, Christ, Son of Mary, the
Great Abbot, the Father, the Son, and the Holy Ghost. [80]

Which, perhaps, reflects Columba's belief that, behind the earthly
battles with pagans, were spiritual battles in the heavenly realms. For
the whole spiritual world, the world of God and Satan, angels and
devils, was very real to Celtic Christians.

Patrick's Breastplate, for example, includes the lines:

I rise today with the power of God to pilot me...
God's host to deliver me:
From snares of devils, from evil temptations,
From nature's failings, from all who wish to harm me,
far or near, alone and in a crowd.
Around me I gather today all these powers:
against every cruel and merciless force to attack my body and soul,
against the charms of false prophets, the black laws of
paganism,
the false laws of heretics, the deceptions of idolatry,
against spells cast by women, smiths and druids,
and all unlawful knowledge that harms the body and soul.[81]

Plenty of similar prayers for protection survive, including several in
which prayer is addressed not only to God but also to saints or angels
or both. *The Saints' Calendar of Adamnán*, for example:

The saints of the four seasons, I long to pray to them...
The saints of the beautiful autumn, I call upon a company not
unharmonious,

---

[79] from Columba's *Altus Prosator*, in Davies, *Celtic Spirituality*, p 410
[80] from the song '*M'Oenuran*', in Bamford and Marsh, *Celtic Christianity: Ecology
and Holiness*, p 110
[81] from *Patrick's Breastplate*, in Davies, *Celtic Spirituality*, p 119

That they may draw near to me, with Mary and Michael...
The saints of the winter I pray to, may they be with me
against the throng of demons...
I beseech the saints of the earth, I beseech all the angels,
I beseech God himself, both when rising and lying down,
Whatever I do or say, that I may dwell in the heavenly land.[82]

Perhaps the most striking example is Ultán's Hymn to Brigit:

Brigit, woman ever excellent, golden, radiant flame,
Lead us to the eternal kingdom, the brilliant, dazzling sun.
May Brigit guide us past crowds of devils,
May she break before us the attack of every plague...
One of the columns of the land with Patrick preeminent,
The adornment above, the royal queen...
We pray to Brigit by the praise of Christ
That we may be worthy of the heavenly kingdom. [83]

Clearly, for any evangelical Christian, this is the less welcome face of early Celtic Christianity!

But for the present I am simply intent on description; the evaluation will have to wait for the final chapter. Suffice it to say that Celtic Christians at least seem to have lived what they believed. Their love for Jesus Christ resulted in lives characterised by earnest discipleship, love of the scriptures, commitment to prayer, costly evangelism and the pursuit of holiness.

What then do modern 'Celtic' Christians believe and practise?

---

[82] *The Saints' Calendar of Adamnán*, an old Irish poem in Davies, *Celtic Spirituality*, p 263f
[83] from *Ultán's Hymn* in Davies, *Celtic Spirituality*, p 121; the hymn is 7th century or later.

5. A Survey of Modern Celtic Sources

Again, the following is not intended to be a comprehensive survey; rather it is simply an attempt to highlight those sources which are most influential today.

5.1. The Carmina Gadelica

In the second half of the nineteenth century one Alexander Carmichael travelled around the Scottish highlands and islands collecting orally transmitted Celtic songs, poems and prayers. The result was published, in six volumes, in 1900, and is still enormously influential. It provides the basic source material for many popular modern 'Celtic' anthologies.

The *Carmina* is a fascinating and impressive collection, and its contents may well be early, but, sadly, it is impossible for us to determine *how* early. Nor can we know with any certainty what effect the intervening years have had on the form, language, and emphases of what may originally have been early Celtic works.

Certainly it is possible to detect early Celtic characteristics. There are prayers here, for example, for every detail of ordinary life: for waking up, washing, getting dressed, lighting the fire, going to work, milking the cow, baking the bread, cooking and eating, weaving, rowing a boat, putting out the fire at night and going to bed. But there are also ways in which the prayers in the *Carmina* differ from those in collections of authentic early Celtic prayers. There is, for example, a higher proportion of prayers to the saints, and especially to Mary, which may testify more to later years of Roman Catholicism than to early Celtic origins. And, although there is a considerable amount of 'nature poetry' in the *Carmina*, it tends to be more sentimental than a study of early Celtic spirituality would lead us to expect.

5.2.   The Iona Community

The Iona Community was established in 1938 by George MacLeod, who began rebuilding the then derelict (Benedictine) Abbey. It describes itself as "a dispersed Christian ecumenical community working for peace and social justice, the rebuilding of community and the renewal of worship."[84] Its liturgy is largely inspired by the *Carmina Gadelica*. It emphasises the goodness of the created world, but pays little attention to the realities of sin and judgement.[85] There is a strong emphasis on music, poetry and the creative arts. The Iona publishing house is Wild Goose publications (the wild goose being, supposedly, a Celtic symbol for the Holy Spirit).

5.3.   The Community of Aidan and Hilda

The Community of Aidan and Hilda, founded in 1994, is a charismatic, ecumenical, renewal community dispersed throughout the world but based at 'The Open Gate' on the island of Lindisfarne. There is a strong Rule of Life demanding study, prayer, evangelism, wholeness and concern for God's creation. The community provides retreats and other events, and a wide range of resources 'for the emerging and existent churches', including an e-learning package. It aims to relate the Celtic Church to God's purposes today, applying early patterns and methods to renew today's church and society. Ray Simpson, a charismatic Anglican and the 'founding guardian' of the community, is the author of *A Pilgrim Way: New Celtic Monasticism for Everyday People* (Kevin Mayhew, 2005).

5.4.   The Lindisfarne Community

Also based on the island of Lindisfarne are the Lindisfarne Community, a group living a 'new form of monasticism.' It is spread across several countries, with a focus on meditation, prayer, study

---

[84]   From the homepage of the Iona Community website, www.iona.org.uk
[85]   for an example, see chapter 6

and Christian service. They view themselves as an 'emerging' church, for the 21ˢᵗ century, emphasising inclusiveness and egalitarian ideals.

The Lindisfarne Scriptorium, founded by an artist, Mary Fleeson, promote Celtic inspired artwork and describe their aim as "to offer an artform which draws the viewer into an experience of prayer, meditation and blessing."

David Adam was vicar of Lindisfarne for thirteen years; he has written widely on Celtic Christianity, including several volumes of Celtic style poetry and prayers such as *The Edge of Glory*, *The Open Gate*, and *Tides and Seasons* (all Triangle/SPCK).

5.5. The Northumbria Community

The Northumbria Community, established in 1992, is a dispersed and "strongly ecumenical" group living a 'missional' form of the 'new monasticism,' and with "an identity rooted in the history and spiritual heritage of Celtic Northumbria." Their mother house is 'Nether Springs', near Felton in Northumberland. The community's Rule is summed up on its website as "availability and vulnerability,"[86] and members use two daily Office books which include traditional Celtic prayers. One of their members is Andy Raine, who has edited a collection entitled *Celtic Daily Prayer: Inspirational Prayers and Readings from the Northumbria Community* (Collins, 2000).

Martin Wallace was chaplain to the seventh century Celtic chapel of St Peter in Bradwell-on-Sea. His *Celtic Resource Book* (Church House, 1998) suggests how Celtic Christianity may function today. It has sections on liturgy, prayer, lessons from the saints, meditation, artistic activities and pilgrimage. He claims Celtic roots for (eg) a love of the natural world, sensitive evangelism, independence of authority structures and uplifting, positive experiences of poetry and prayer.

---

[86] www.northumbriacommunity.org

5.6.   The Anamchara Fellowship

The Anamchara Fellowship is another of the "new expressions of monasticism, founded in the tradition of the Episcopal Church, with a Celtic spirit." Their website says, "We strive to be an inclusive community, welcoming men and women, clergy and lay, married, single or partners in a committed relationship... we are bound to each other by common ideals and a commitment to prayer and service. Our primary ministries focus on catechesis, pastoral care and spiritual direction." Members take vows of simplicity, fidelity and obedience, and pilgrimage to 'Celtic' sites is a key feature.

5.7.   Others

There is a whole host of very eclectic groups, of which the following is fairly typical:

> New Tara' describes its purpose as providing "an inter-Traditional and interdenominational environment opened to anyone who is drawn toward the Celtic spiritual and religious life, be it Pagan, Reconstructionist, Traditionalist, Christian, Christo-pagan, Druidic, Wiccan, or any other form of Celtic or Celtic-inspired spirituality. [87]

Finally, it may be useful to some to know that Ian Bradley has a fairly comprehensive survey of twentieth century writers on Celtic Christianity in chapter 6 of his *Celtic Christianity: Making Myths and Chasing Dreams.*[88]

---

[87]   Brian Walsh, "New Tara", online at http://www.newtara.org
[88]   Ian Bradley, *Celtic Christianity: Making Myths and Chasing Dreams* (Edinburgh: EUP, 1999)

6. Distinctive Features of Contemporary Celtic Christianity

As the above survey will perhaps have indicated, it is almost impossible to ascribe any consistent theology to contemporary Celtic spirituality, because the interest groups are so many and so varied: from modern druid to New Age to professedly Christian. Even if we restrict ourselves to this last, it still encompasses a wide variety of different emphases and perspectives. Broadly speaking, however, there are two groups: in the one are those who maintain that true Celtic Christianity is, at least for the most part, biblically orthodox; in the other are those who in some way, and to varying extents, 'reinvent' it. This chapter will largely focus on that second, and larger, group. In common with much 21st century religion, they tend to reject a rational and objective approach in favour of a more emotional and subjective one. Mackey, for example, makes no apology for describing his criterion for determining authentic Celtic Christianity as "whatever seems to reverberate with some depths of my own Celtic consciousness."[89]

And, in terms of sources, Bradley rightly points out that, rather than working from early texts, many 'modern interpretations stem from 1960s reworkings of nineteenth century anthologies' (chiefly the *Carmina Gaedelica*).

Add to this the fact that each author emphasises their own particular interest. So, for example, Doherty emphasises the community nature of Celtic Christianity (as against our contemporary

---

[89] James P. Mackey, *An Introduction to Celtic Christianity*, (Edinburgh: T & T Clark, 1995), p 10

individualism)[90]; De Waal focuses on its holistic nature (as against our contemporary fragmented, materialistic society)[91], and so on.

Perhaps, then, the only safe generalisations we can make are that the emphasis tends to be on practice (style of prayer, artwork, soul friends, conservation, pilgrimage etc) rather than belief, that the result inevitably tends towards both syncretism and sentimentality, and that, where there is a degree of theological agreement, it is found in the avoidance of those 'unpalatable' elements of Celtic Christianity which emphasise sin and penance, judgment and hell (as in O'Donoghue, James, Hull).

Consider for example, the following modern comments on Celtic beliefs:

> O'Donoghue: the Celts lacked "that indelible sense of sinfulness and divine wrath that we find in some other Christian traditions."[92]

> James: "Not for the Celtic saints of that heroic age chilling and childish depictions of hell and eternal damnation, and little for them of mortal sin and original sin. It seems that they spoke rather of the sweetness and beauty of this life on Earth."[93]

I trust that the departure from what we've seen of original Celtic thinking is already transparent.

O'Donoghue defends his view by asserting that Christianity became "wedded to nature and the natural world" in early Celtic

---

[90] Jerry Doherty, *A Celtic Model of Ministry: The Reawakening of Community Spirituality,* (Collegeville, Minnesota: Liturgical Press, 2003)

[91] Esther De Waal, *A World Made Whole: Rediscovering the Celtic Tradition,* (London: Fount, 1991)

[92] Noel O'Donoghue, *The Mountain behind the Mountain: Aspects of the Celtic Tradition,* (Edinburgh: T & T Clark, 1993), p 38

[93] C. James, *An Age of Saints: Its Relevance for Us Today,* (Lampeter: 1996), p 95f

thinking, just as it was wedded to the law in Rome and the logos in Hellenism.[94]

Eleanor Hull contrasts the (supposed) attitude of Bernard of Clairvaux with that of a 'typical' Irish monk. She imagines them both walking round Lake Geneva; Bernard oblivious to the natural beauty because he was preoccupied with "sin and repentance, the fall and redemption, hell and heaven", whereas the Irish monk "showed no such inclination and suffered no such terrors", because he was preoccupied with the goodness of nature and "refused to mingle the idea of evil with what God had made so good."[95]

It is not surprising that such authors are averse to thinking of sin and salvation in forensic terms. They much prefer a therapeutic view, and point to Cummean's description of sins as "wounds which need remedies"[96] as if that were the only Celtic treatment of sin. Where redemption is mentioned, it tends to be in terms of restoring a sin-tainted creation to its right relationship with God. Bradley, for example, suggests that understanding the atonement in forensic language is alien to Celtic Christianity, and that it should instead be understood in terms of liberation and completion.[97] The consequences are inevitable:

> Sin is a disruption in a relationship; the most positive way to address such disruption is by analogy with sickness rather than law. Thus God is acknowledged as creator and healer in contrast to ruler and law-giver.[98]

---

[94] O'Donoghue, *The Mountain behind the Mountain,* p 14

[95] Eleanor Hull, *The Poem Book of the Gael: Translations from Irish Gaelic Poetry into English Prose and Verse* (orig. pub. Chatto & Windus, 1912, repubd. Whitefish, US: Kessinger, 1993), p 20

[96] *The Penitential of Cummean* in Davies, *Celtic Spirituality,* p.230; compare the quotes on sin in chapter 3.

[97] Ian Bradley, *The Celtic Way* (London: DLT, 1993), p 65

[98] Thomas O'Loughlin, *Journeys on the Edges: The Celtic Tradition* (London: DLT, 2000), p 112

In other words, a false dichotomy is created within the very nature of God.

Hull, O'Donoghue and others make it clear that their views are based on the belief that Celtic theology was heavily influenced by Pelagius. As a result, in places at least, their books read like an attempt to rehabilitate Pelagius at Augustine's expense. Ian Bradley, for example, writing on redemption, explicitly contrasts the Catholic and Protestant 'negative' Augustinian view with the purportedly 'positive' Celtic view. Matthew Fox even suggests we "jettison the whole doctrine of original sin and develop a new theology which celebrates the goodness of creation."[99] The result is not only an unbiblically low view of sin and salvation, but an equally unbiblically high view of creation.

So, for example, Bradley strongly advocates replacing the view that human nature is corrupt, degenerate, and "radically tainted by sin and evil" with a view of human nature that is "full of potential and opportunity, longing for completion and perfection".[100] Doherty likewise characterises modern secular society as "basically good and law abiding but eager for spiritual growth,"[101] thus reducing the need for either proclamation or conversion. One consequence of such belief in the 'essential goodness' of human nature is the fact that several of the 'new monastic' Rules fail to reflect the asceticism of their Celtic heroes.[102] Another is the transformation of the *anamchara* from "stringent physician of the soul" to "little more than a spiritual chum."[103]

Mackey describes the Celtic view of the natural world as "altogether good and salvific... This natural world... is good through and through as the Genesis refrain insists." That word 'salvific' is

[99] Matthew Fox, *Original Blessing: A Primer in Creation Spirituality* (first pub 1983, repub. NY: Tarcher/Putnam, 2000); cited in Bradley, *The Celtic Way*, p 51
[100] Bradley, *The Celtic Way*, p 60
[101] Doherty, *A Celtic Model of Ministry*, p 100
[102] for example, the *Rule* of the Northumbria Community; see chapter 5
[103] Donald Meek, *The Quest for Celtic Christianity* (Edinburgh: Handsel, 2000), p 97

significant, for Mackey believes the Celts viewed the natural world as more than simply good; he believes they considered it "the locus of the gracious power of God."[104]

For many 'contemporary Celts', this 'gracious power of God' in nature is experienced primarily as revelation. They talk of creation in almost sacramental terms, as communicating the Word of God[105], as a 'book' revealing Him to humankind[106]. But some writers go further and maintain that God is not simply revealed through creation but is incarnate in creation.[107]

So Bradley maintains that the Celts believed "God is to be found both within creation and outside it," and clearly approves of that understanding[108].

Noel O'Donoghue interprets Patrick's idea of 'Christ the true sun' not as a metaphor but as "a medium through which he shines".[109]

David Adam speaks of a "creation personally united with its Creator in every atom and fibre," adding, "creation was the means of communion with Father, Son and Holy Spirit.... [The Celts] saw a universe ...suffused with a Presence that calls, nods and beckons"[110]

Michael Mitton speaks of the Celtic "expectation of meeting God in his creation".[111]

And Martin Wallace includes the following 'prayer', from a syncretistic mediaeval source,[112] in his *Celtic Resource Book*:

[104] Mackey, *An Introduction to Celtic Christianity*, p 12
[105] O'Loughlin, *Journeys on the Edges*, p 45
[106] Sheldrake, *Living between Two Worlds*, p 73
[107] Meek and others attribute this to contemporary 'Celtic Christianity' rejecting the perceived Cartesian divorce between spirit and matter. See Meek, *The Quest*, p 69f
[108] Bradley, *The Celtic Way*, p 35
[109] O'Donoghue, *The Mountain behind the Mountain*, p.14; cf Patrick's *Confession*, para 60, in Davies, *Celtic Spirituality*, p 83
[110] David Adam, *The Eye of the Eagle: Meditations on the Hymn 'Be Thou my Vision'* (London: Triangle/SPCK, 1990), p 7
[111] Mitton, *Restoring the Woven Cord*, p 56

I am the wind that breathes upon the sea,
I am the wave on the ocean,
I am the murmur of waves rustling,
I am the rays of the sun,
I am the beam of the moon and stars,
I am the power of trees growing,
I am the bud breaking into blossom,
I am the movement of the salmon swimming,
I am the courage of the wild boar fighting,
I am the speed of the stag running,
I am the strength of the ox pulling the plough,
I am the size of the mighty oak tree,
And I am the thoughts of all people
Who praise my beauty and grace. [113]

Richard Woods advocates reclaiming this "ancient contemplative heritage of experiencing nature as theophany."[114] Bradley cites the monk Thomas Merton, who, in his Celtic spirituality, found "God in nature" and "the validity of other religions, notably Hinduism and Buddhism."[115] And liberal commentators such as John Macquarrie and Matthew Fox urge us to rehabilitate that ninth century Irishman, John Scottus Eriugena, whose neoplatonist-inspired works established the created world as a theophany.

This approach clearly leads to panentheism and thus to the veneration, or even worship, of the natural world itself.

Not surprising then, to find that contemporary Celtic spirituality acknowledges the concept of holy places. Toulson writes that the "caves, holy wells and ruined oratories associated with the Celtic saints are... numinous in themselves."[116] Nor to find that

---

[112] 'The Black Book of Carmarthen', a 13th century Welsh MS which appears to combine Christian with earlier pagan material.
[113] Wallace, The Celtic Resource Book, p 58
[114] Richard J. Woods, The Spirituality of the Celtic Saints (NY: Orbis, 2000), p 183
[115] Bradley, The Celtic Way, p 113
[116] Shirley Toulson, The Celtic Year (Rockport, MA: Element, 1995), p 9

'pilgrimage' to 'holy' sites such as Iona or Lindisfarne, has become popular. The Anamchara Fellowship, for example, considers pilgrimage to be "the single most important expression of Celtic Christianity."[117] We must note however, that much contemporary pilgrimage has more in common with a tourist trip than with the original Celtic concept. Certainly, there is rarely much penance involved, rarely much asceticism, and rarely much missionary fervour. 'Pilgrimage' has been somewhat romanticised.

Not surprising, either, to find that the 'green' movement has enthusiastically embraced this modern version of 'Celtic' spirituality, and that, in return, contemporary Celtic Christianity of all kinds has a significant environmental emphasis, encouraging its adherents to relate to the earth as 'partners not oppressors'. Ray Simpson urges: "We need to cherish it, give it rest, respect its nature and its rhythms and to bless it."[118]

And the Iona Community Worship book includes the following 'closing responses' in its liturgy:

Leader: This we know, the earth does not belong to us,

All: We belong to the earth.

Leader: This we know, all things are connected,

All: Like the blood that unites one family.

Leader: This we know, we did not weave the web of life,

All: We are merely a strand in it.

Leader: This we know, whatever we do to the web,

All: We do to ourselves.

Leader: Let us give thanks for the gift of creation,

---

[117] Anamchara Fellowship, "Pilgrimage", online at http://www.anamcharafellowship.org/pilgrimage.htm
[118] Ray Simpson, *Celtic Spirituality: Rhythm, Roots and Relationships*, p 15

All: **Let us give thanks that all things hold together in Christ.** [119]

In the words, 'whatever we do to the web, we do to ourselves', this Iona liturgy introduces a further, related, characteristic of much contemporary Celtic Christianity, which is usually expressed via the concepts of 'oneness' and 'interrelatedness'. The suggestion is that the early Christian Celts saw everything – material and spiritual – as circular and interconnected.[120] "This we know: all things are connected, like the blood that unites one family." Many different conclusions are drawn from this so-called 'knowledge':

For Jerry Docherty it explains why there was no division in their minds between sacred and secular, a feature we have already noticed in Celtic prayers.[121] It also explains why they found the idea of the Trinity so attractive – because the idea of a Godhead who was "one in Trinity of Persons"[122] would chime well with the idea of the interconnectedness of all things.

For Esther De Waal it encourages her to see in Celtic Christianity the possiblilty of the "world made whole." "What we gain from a rediscovery of the Celtic tradition", she writes, is

> the inter-relationship and the inter-connectedness of all things...all those dualities of heart and mind, of time and eternity, of East and West, of pagan and Christian, of the inner and the outer all come under the sway of a creator God whose all-inclusive love allows everything the freedom to be itself and yet also brings all together into one whole. [123]

---

[119] From 'A Creation Liturgy' in *The Iona Community Worship Book* (Wild Goose Publications, 1991)
[120] This is said to be reflected in their characteristic 'knotwork' art.
[121] Doherty, *A Celtic Model of Ministry*, p 33; cf chapter 4 of this booklet.
[122] Ibid., p 40
[123] De Waal, *A World made Whole*, p 129

This is a classic example of the contemporary perception that early Celtic Christians were tolerant of pagan beliefs and happy to assimilate pagan culture.[124]

For some it means that Celtic spirituality today recognizes the fragmentation of the Church over the intervening years, and offers a way of bringing denominations back together again, "to heal a fragmented world."[125]

For many it means the repudiation of all social barriers of gender and sexuality.

So, for example, the Iona community celebrates its inclusiveness with the words "We believe in the sacredness of all human relationships... about 10% of our staff are gay, lesbian, bisexual or transgender. They are fully and openly part of our common life."[126]

It is worth saying a little more about the 'repudiation of all social barriers of gender', because this is such a strong feature of so much contemporary Celtic spirituality. It is rooted, not only in the idea of interconnected 'oneness' but also in the perceptions that original Celtic Christianity accorded women an "unusually high status" [127] and "had little time for hierarchical ecclesiastical order."[128] Bray and others argue that these perceptions are spurious and that the situation of Celtic women was in fact much the same as that of women in other Northern European cultures at the time.[129]

Nonetheless, contemporary Celtic spirituality looks to positive female examples like Hilda, the abbess of Whitby in Northumbria,

---

[124] Columba's 'My Druid is Christ' is often cited in support of this perception; see chapter 4 of this booklet.

[125] Simpson, *Celtic Spirituality*, p 5

[126] Iona Community, "Sexuality", online at http://www.iona.org.uk/sexuality.php

[127] Bray, "Celtic Spirituality: Its Origins and Interpretations", in *Churchman* vol 114:3, 2000, p 258

[128] Meek, *The Quest*, p 87; see also Bradley, *Celtic Christianity*, p 217

[129] Bray, "Celtic Spirituality: Its Origins and Interpretations", p 259

and finds therein not only encouraging models for female church leadership but, in some cases, the justification for a degree of feminist pride which Hilda herself would have been the first to repudiate. Mitton is one who cites several examples, and he is not alone in suggesting that the Celts were "more at ease with human sexuality" generally than the Roman churches.[130]

To sum up, then: concepts of 'oneness' and 'interrelatedness' result in an emphasis on Trinity, ecumenism, syncretism, feminism, and tolerance within many versions of contemporary Celtic Christianity.

In 1997, Clifford Longley, in the *Daily Telegraph*, summarised the whole movement as "ecological, feminist, spontaneous, non-cerebral, poetic, mystical, almost pantheistic," noting that it "easily shades off into New Age paganism."[131] Martin Reith scathingly described it as "easy and self-indulgent... twee, drawing room religion."[132]

Yet there are many who insist that this theologically open, all-embracing kind of 'Christianity' is just "the kind of reality we seem to need today."[133]

But, as should by now be evident, I believe they are fooling themselves and others by calling this 'Celtic Christianity,' for it is a far cry from the kind of Christianity espoused by Patrick, Columba, Hilda, Aidan and Columbanus. It has strayed a long way from its moorings in biblical orthodoxy.

Some generously attribute this to romanticism, to "wistful attempts to recapture a golden age of spiritual wholeness."[134] Others,

---

[130] Mitton, *Restoring the Woven Cord*, p 118
[131] Clifford Longley, "Is it time for a backlash against Celtic Christianity?" in *The Daily Telegraph*, 31 Jan, 1997.
[132] from an interview between Martin Reith and Ian Bradley, cited in Bradley, *Celtic Christianity*, p 194
[133] Bamford & Marsh, *Celtic Christianity: Ecology and Holiness*, p 10
[134] Culling, *What is Celtic Christianity?*, p 4

less generously, attribute it to a careless approach to the historical evidence, or simply to subjective sentimentality. Whatever the cause, the result is error.

We've already noted the attempts to rehabilitate men like Pelagius and Eriugena, but other errors abound too. Bradley, for example, clearly favours the Moltmannian idea that we replace "our rather static view of God with a much more dynamic picture of a continuous creator who is constantly reaching out in love."[135] And Mitton, with very little evidence, confidently assures us that the early Celts would have approved of John Wimber's 'power evangelism'![136]

Thus the phrase 'Celtic spirituality' is easily emptied of reliable content.

Meek summarises the situation well, except that he under-emphasises the focus on prayer for grace:

> The concepts which are less attractive in our own age, but which lie at the heart of early Christianity in the Celtic lands – a heavy emphasis on judgement, retribution, penance, self-denial and mortification... leading to (sometimes) severe asceticism, which may well have been the real distinguishing features of this form of Christian devotion – have been removed, played down, or nicely romanticised... 'Celtic Christianity'... looks good, feels soothing, and is even attractive to the outside world, but it is not necessarily 'real' or true to its name.[137]

Clearly any truly biblical evangelical needs to tread very warily through this minefield, for it has become abundantly clear that, in writing as they do, some are presenting 'Celtic Christianity' as a viable alternative to mainstream Christian orthodoxy. A more faithful representation of early Celtic Christianity would render such attempts impossible.

---

[135] Bradley, *The Celtic Way*, p 43
[136] Mitton, *Restoring the Woven Cord*, p 93
[137] Meek, *The Quest*, p 242f

7.   Light from Dark Ages?

Contemporary 'Celtic' Christianity is, then, a mixture of reality and romanticism, heterodoxy and orthodoxy, rediscovery and reinvention. Such a situation is hardly surprising in the 'itching ears'[138] atmosphere of our postmodern world, but it does make it very difficult to produce any overall assessment. Therefore this chapter will focus on the early form of Celtic Christianity and the critique will only apply to contemporary versions insofar as they accurately reflect that original.

As we have seen, the early Celtic churches were not <u>that</u> separate or different from the Roman churches, and they shared many of the same problems. Therefore, in the process of assessment, we must take particular care not to read back into those early years either the errors of later medieval Catholicism or the characteristics of the Catholic church today, whether in Ireland or further afield. After all, these were the years before papal infallibility, clerical celibacy, auricular confession, transubstantiation, the canonisation of saints (initiated in 995 AD), the teaching that tradition was equal in authority with scripture and so on...

What then are we to make of Celtic Christianity?

7.1.   The Word of God and prayer.

The Celtic love for the Bible and prayer is rightly stressed in contemporary Celtic spirituality.

Their hermeneutical methods, especially the more allegorical ones, may have been questionable (to put it mildly!), but they did aim to practise wholeheartedly whatever they found in scripture and were not prone to excising portions which didn't suit them. Some of their

---

[138]   see 2 Timothy 4:3

prayers, especially those directed to the saints, may have been questionable, but they were seeking to imitate exemplary lives[139], and they did love to spend time in thankful, honest, practical and earnest prayer.

Maybe we can usefully learn, like the Celts, to love simply reading the Bible (as well as studying it), and humbly to accept whatever we find therein, albeit with rather more attention to hermeneutics.

Maybe we can usefully learn to delight in prayer as much as preaching, and to balance our intercessions with more thankfulness for all the Lord's kindnesses, and more genuine contrition in our confessions.

7.2. *God and creation*

The Celtic focus on both the transcendence and immanence of God is rarely reflected in contemporary Celtic spirituality, although their Trinitarian emphasis usually is. Getting the balance right is a vital foundation for true biblical spirituality. Err in one direction, and the Lord may seem too despairingly distant; err in the other direction and we may succumb to complacent, irreverent over-familiarity.

The Celtic love for the natural world is very often overstated. Certainly they did appreciate creation but they did not confuse the Creator with his creation. Certainly they did praise God for the natural world, but they also prayed for protection from its dangers and threats. Consider, for example, the ninth century prayer of St Sanctan:

> May Christ save us from every bloody death, from fire, from raging sea... may the Lord each hour come to me against wind, against swift waters.[140]

---

[139] along the lines of Paul's instruction in Philippians 3:17
[140] cited by Márkus, "The End of Celtic Christianity", p 52

Furthermore, they clearly did believe they had a God-given dominion over creation, and sometimes wielded that dominion without due thought for the consequences. The law tracts of early Ireland, for example, reveal the need to legislate for the protection of trees, because so many were being cut down to build monasteries.[141] Thus we must conclude, with Márkus, that "the view of happy Celts living in perfect harmony with nature is totally unrealistic."[142]

In fact, even Bradley admits that, as a result of studying Celtic poetry, he has had to revise his thinking with regard to the Celtic attitude to creation.[143] He now accepts that the early Celtic Christians were less 'green' than is commonly believed.

Nonetheless, the Celtic attitude to the natural world, like the Bible's attitude to the natural world, was more positive than seems to be the case for many 21st century evangelicals (still influenced as we are by the dualism of Greek philosophy). Contemporary Celtic Christianity may overplay creation at the expense of redemption, but our tendency is commonly to err in the opposite direction. So much so that it is secular groupings like Friends of the Earth who have the reputation for enjoying creation and caring for it. But there is little point in redemption without creation. And a strong doctrine of creation, provided it remains biblical, will only improve our understanding of redemption. It will challenge our consumerist individualism and help us to see the 'big picture' of our Lord's saving purposes.[144] So maybe we could usefully learn, like the Celts, to be more appreciative of creation, to be more thankful for it, to care for it in obedience to the Creator's command, to rejoice in it and thereby to give Him glory for it. Furthermore, if Mike Raiter is correct in observing that a 'quest for connectedness' with the natural world is a

---

[141] Meek, *The Quest*, p 92
[142] Márkus, "The End of Celtic Christianity", p 52
[143] Bradley, *Celtic Christianity*, p 228
[144] see, for example, Psalms 97, 104, Romans 8

key part of modern spirituality[145], then the Celts' example in this respect may even have direct significance for our evangelism.

7.3. Sin and salvation

Correspondingly, the Celtic belief in the 'essential goodness' of human nature is frequently overplayed in contemporary Celtic spirituality, for, as we have seen, 'weighty themes' such as sin, repentance and judgement are very prominent in early Celtic writings. Indeed the sinfulness of human nature was "the greatest single reason for practicing penance."[146]

We have also noticed, in Celtic prayers and, especially throughout Patrick's *Confession*, an equally strong emphasis on grace. But what of the cross? Clearly the place of the cross is key to the evaluation of any professedly Christian spirituality. And we have to accept that, though the cross features large in much Celtic literature, the way the Celts call for the protection of the cross, especially in some of the *loricae* (Breastplate prayers), can seem somewhat talismanic and superstitious. For example, the prayer known as *Alexander's Breastplate* contains the lines:

> Christ's cross is bright, a shining breastplate
> against all harm and against our enemies,
> may it be strong: the place of our protection.[147]

Nonetheless, the aversion of Bradley and others to forensic language on the grounds that it is alien to the Celts is historically unfair. After all, the Celts were not attempting to *explain* the atonement in any language. We can say that they clearly believed sin must be punished, and that the cross provided 'protection' from the consequences of sin. We can say that they were lovers of biblical orthodoxy, and biblically, while the cross is liberating and healing, it

---

[145] Mike Raiter, *Stirrings of the Soul: Evangelicals and the New Spirituality* (London: Good Book Co, 2004), p 36f
[146] this point is argued by Meek in *The Quest*, pp 83-96
[147] from *Alexander's Breastplate* in Davies, *Celtic Spirituality*, p 270

is also, and primarily, propitiatory. We simply cannot say much beyond that.

As for the penitential system, there are undoubtedly dangers associated with it. As we have seen, it could, and sometimes did, lead to a belief in salvation by works, a corresponding denial of grace, and thus a host of problems with regard to assurance. On the other hand, at best, it could simply reflect a sincere and earnest commitment to 'deny oneself, take up the cross, and follow Christ.' Certainly Matthew 16:24 seems to have been a favourite verse of the Celts.[148]

So, while we may not wish to emulate the Celts' strict asceticism or penances, maybe we could usefully learn, like them, to be more serious about the problem of continuing sin in our lives and to be more disciplined about our discipleship. How often are we moved to tears by our own sin? Have we even considered the possible value of spiritual disciplines other than prayer and Bible reading – for example fasting or biblical meditation? And we may not choose to call them 'soul friends', but surely it is a good idea for all Christians to have a friend with whom to discuss their spiritual growth and health?

7.4. *Mission and evangelism*

The Celtic zeal for evangelism is frequently watered down in contemporary Celtic spirituality, and they are often portrayed as syncretistic compromisers with paganism. In fact, as we have seen, they were far from tolerant of pagan beliefs and far from reticent about the 'less palatable' gospel realities of sin, judgment and hell. Their motives may have been more penitential than we would expect in an itinerant evangelist today; nevertheless, many were, without doubt, impressively successful missionaries. Perhaps Columba's 'My Druid is Christ' should be cited more often within its original context:

Alone am I upon the mountain;...

---

[148] see, for example, the commentary on that verse in *Catechesis Celtica*, in Davies, *Celtic Spirituality*, pp 363-365

I have no more fear of aught
than if there were six thousand with me....
Whatever God destines for one,
He shall not go from the world till it befall him;...
O Living God, O Living God!
Woe to him who for any reason does evil...
Our fortune does not depend on sneezing.
Nor on a bird on the point of a crooked tree...
Better is he on whom we depend,
The Father, – the One – and the Son...
I reverence not the voices of birds,
nor sneezing, nor any charm in the wide world,...
My druid is Christ, the Son of God...[149]

In other words, it seems that Columba was simply trying to communicate that Christ had replaced the druids in his devotion. Furthermore, the 'Christianising' of some elements of pagan culture was less distinctively Celtic than is sometimes made out. Bede, for example, records a letter sent from Pope Gregory to Abbot Mellitus in which Gregory advises that pagan temples should be rededicated to the Lord instead of destroyed and that Christian feast days should replace pagan ones. He makes it clear that this is his deliberate strategy, so that the English

> will more readily come to desire the joys of the Spirit. For it is certainly impossible to eradicate all errors from obstinate minds at one stroke, and whoever wishes to climb to a mountain top climbs gradually step by step, and not in one leap.[150]

So, while not wishing in any way to compromise the gospel, maybe we could usefully learn, like the Celts, to be more culturally sensitive

---

[149] from the poem *M'Oenuran*, available at www.chasingcolumba.wordpress.com Sneezing and various natural phenomena all had superstitious 'spiritual' significance in druidic religion.

[150] Bede, *Ecclesiastical History of the English People*, Bk 1:30, p 92

and adaptable in our evangelism as well as to be more zealous and self-sacrificial in our missionary work generally.

7.5. *'Oneness' and its implications (or not...)*

The alleged Celtic belief in ecumenism, feminism, and tolerance is frequently paraded in contemporary Celtic spirituality. In fact, all three are, to use Donald Meek's rather telling phrase, "figments of contemporary counter-cultural imagination".[151]

With regard to feminism, we have already observed that the situation of Celtic women was much the same as that of non-Celtic women of the period. Women could and did reach positions of some status, and thus do provide models of female leadership, but, in Ireland at least, the law still restricted their freedoms.[152]

With regard to tolerance of all human relationships, it is difficult to reconcile the inclusive attitude of some of the 'new monastic' communities with, for example, the penances prescribed for homosexuality by the *Penitential of Cummean*.[153]

With regard to ecumenism, there is considerable evidence of power struggles between various churches and clergy during the first millennium, as evidenced by the need for the Synod of Whitby or the insistence of Armagh that she took precedence among the Irish churches.[154] Those who look back beyond the "painful separation" of the Reformation in order to find their roots in a more peaceable Celtic church will only discover other divisions. Maybe we could usefully learn not to read our 21st century interests back into previous ages, and not to expect a 'perfect church' in any age!

---

[151] Meek, *The Quest*, p 120
[152] see Fergus Kelly, *A Guide to Early Irish Law* (Dublin, 1988), p 76f; cited by Meek, *The Quest*, p 119
[153] *The Penitential of Cummean*, in Davies, *Celtic Spirituality*, p 242
[154] *Liber Angeli* 13.18, in Bieler, L. (ed.) *The Patrician Texts in the Book of Armagh* (Dublin, 1979), p 186

7.6.   Lifestyle and aesthetics.

The Celts' practical faith, and especially their artistic skills - poetry, music, painting and craftwork – are also very much at the forefront of contemporary Celtic spirituality. Evangelicals, by contrast, tend to be more inclined toward a cerebral, 'left-brained' approach to the Christian faith. Maybe we could learn, like the Celts, a greater appreciation of beauty, poetry and artistry. Maybe we could then communicate the gospel more effectively to less cerebral, 'right-brained' people.

Maybe we could learn too from their simplicity of living, which challenges 21st century consumerism, their 'down to earth' community-based lifestyle, which challenges 21st century self-legislative individualism, and even their love of celibacy, which challenges our 21st century assumptions concerning sexuality.

So did 'the light of the glorious gospel of Christ' shine as brightly in those 'dark' Celtic ages? Yes, I believe it did. Not perfectly, of course. There are errors to be avoided and practices we would be better not to emulate. There were, no doubt, both nominal Christians and false teachers in the churches of the first millennium just as there are in our churches today, and there is unlikely to be much lasting benefit from their legacies. But there was also Patrick, and Columba, and Hilda, and Aidan, and countless others whose love for Christ, love for his Word, love for the lost, passion for holiness and commitment to prayer qualifies them as 'heroes of faith'. Their example is of benefit to the Church in every age.

> Therefore, since we are surrounded by so great a cloud of witnesses, let us also lay aside every weight and the sin that clings so closely, and let us run with perseverance the race that is set before us, looking to Jesus...[155]

---

[155]   Hebrews 12:1f

Bibliography

Primary Sources:

Adam, D. *The Edge of Glory: Prayers in the Celtic Tradition.* London: Triangle/SPCK, 1985.

Adam, D. *The Open Gate: Celtic Prayers for Growing Spirituality.* London: Triangle/SPCK, 1994.

Adam, D. *Tides and Seasons: Modern Prayers in the Celtic Tradition.* London: Triangle/SPCK, 1989.

Bamford, C. & Marsh, W.P. *Celtic Christianity, Ecology and Holiness* (an anthology of stories, songs and poems). Edinburgh, Floris, 1986 (Repr 1991)

Bieler, L. (ed.) *The Patrician Texts in the Book of Armagh.* Dublin, 1979

Davies, O. & Bowie, F. *Celtic Christian Spirituality: An anthology of Medieval and Modern Sources.* London: SPCK, 1995

Davies & O'Loughlin, T., *Celtic Spirituality* (in the Classics of Western Spirituality series). NY: Paulist Press, 1999

Duffy, J. *Patrick in his own Words.* Dublin: Veritas, 2000

Hull, E. *The Poem Book of the Gael: Translations from Irish Gaelic Poetry into English Prose and Verse.* Whitefish, US: Kessinger, 1993

Hyde, D. *Religious Songs of Connach* (first published 1906) republished Shannon: IUP, 1972

O'Malley, B. *A Celtic Primer: The Complete Celtic Worship Resource and Collection* Norwich: Canterbury. Press, 2002

Raine, Andy (ed) *Celtic Daily Prayer: Inspirational Prayers and Readings from the Northumbria Community.* London: Collins, 2000 (updated 2005)

Reith, M. *God in our Midst: Prayers and Devotions from the Celtic Tradition.* Triangle/SPCK, 1989 (first published 1974)

Robson, P. *A Celtic Liturgy.* London: SPCK, 2008

Walker, G.S.M. (ed) *Sancti Columbani Opera.* Dublin, 1970

Wallace, M. *Celtic Reflections.* Bristol: Tim Tilley, Undated

Wallace, M. *The Celtic Resource Book.* London: Church House, 1998

Secondary Sources:

Adam, D. *Aidan, Bede, Cuthbert: Three Inspirational Saints.* London: Triangle/SPCK 2006

Adam, D. *Fire of the North: the Life of St. Cuthbert.* London: Triangle/SPCK 2008

Adam, D. *The Cry of the Deer.* London: Triangle/SPCK, 1987

Adam, D. *The Eye of the Eagle: Meditations on the Hymn 'Be Thou My Vision'* London: Triangle/SPCK, 1990

Atherton, M. (ed.) *Celts and Christians: New Approaches to the Religious Traditions of Britain and Ireland.* Cardiff: UWP, 2002

Bamford, C. & Marsh, W.P.. *Celtic Christianity: Ecology and Holiness.* Edinburgh, Floris, 1986

Bede, *Ecclesiastical History of the English People.* London: Penguin, 1955

Bradley, I. *Celtic Christianity: Making Myths and Chasing Dreams.* Edinburgh: EUP, 1999

Bradley, I. *The Celtic Way.* London: DLT, 1993

Bradley, I. *Colonies of Heaven: Celtic Models for Today's Church.* London:DLT, 2000

Bray, D.A. 'Celtic Spirituality: Its Origins and Interpretations' in *Churchman* Vol.114:3, 2000, pp. 250-261

Culling, E. *What is Celtic Chrisitanity?* [Grove SS45] Bramcote: Grove 1993

Davies, O & O'Loughlin, T. . *Celtic Spirituality.* Mahwah, NJ: Paulist Press, 1999

De Waal, E. *A World made Whole: Rediscovering the Celtic Tradition.* London: Fount, 1991

De Waal, E. *The Celtic Way of Prayer: The Recovery of the Religious Imagination.* London: H&S, 1996

Doherty, J.C, *A Celtic Model of Ministry: The Reawakening of Community Spirituality.* Collegeville, Minn: Liturgical Press, 2003

Howard, M. *Angels and Goddesses: Celtic Christianity and Paganism in Ancient Britain.* Milverton: Capall Bann, 1993

Letham, R. *The Holy Trinity: In Scripture, History, Theology and Worship,* Phillipsburg, New Jersey P & R, 2004

Mackey, J.P. *An Introduction to Celtic Christianity.* Edin: T&T Clark, 1995

Márkus, G. 'The End of Celtic Christianity' in *Epworth Review* 24 (1997): 45-55

Meek, D.E. *The Quest for Celtic Christianity.* Edin: Handsel, 2000

Meek, D.E. 'Surveying the Saints: Reflections on Recent Writings on 'Celtic Christianity''in *Scottish Bulletin of Evangelical Theology* 15, 1997, pp 50-60

Meek, D.E. 'Celtic Christianity: What is it and when was it?' in *SBET* 9 (1991) pp 13-21

Meek, D.E. 'Modern Celtic Christianity: The Contemporary Revival and its Roots' in *SBET* 10 (1992) pp 6-31

Mitton, M. *Restoring the Woven Cord: Strands of Celtic Christianity for the Church Today.* London: DLT, 1995

O'Donoghue, N.D. *The Mountain behind the Mountain: Aspects of the Celtic Tradition.* Edin: T&T Clark, 1993

O'Donoghue, N.D. *The Angels Keep their Ancient Places.* Edin: T&T Clark, 2001

O'Duinn, S. *Where Three Streams Meet: Celtic Spirituality.* Dublin: Columba, 2000

O'Loughlin, T. *Celtic Theology: Humanity, World and God in Early Irish Writings.* London: Continuum, 2000

O'Loughlin, T. *Journeys on the Edges: The Celtic Tradition.* London: DLT, 2000

Raiter, M. *Stirrings of the Soul: Evangelicals and the New Spirituality.* London: Good Book Co, 2004

Sheldrake, P. *Living Between Two Worlds: Place and Journey in Celtic Spirituality.* London, DLT, 1995

Simpson, R. *Celtic Spirituality: Rhythm, Roots and Relationships* [Grove SS85] Cambridge: Grove, 2003

Simpson, R. *A Pilgrim Way: New Celtic Monasticism for Everyday People.* Kevin Mayhew, 2005

Tristram, K. *The Story of Holy Island.* Norwich: Canterbury Press, 2009

Tristram, K. *Columbanus: the earliest voice of Christian Ireland.* Dublin: Columba Press, 2010

Van de Weyer, R. *Celtic Fire.* London: DLT, 1990

Woods, R.J. *The Spirituality of the Celtic Saints.* NY: Orbis, 2000

Websites:

www.lamp.ac.uk/celtic (the Celtic Christianity e-library

www.iona.org.uk

www.ionabooks.com (Wild Goose publications)

www.celticchristianity.org

www.celticchristianitytoday.org

www.chasingcolumba.wordpress.com

www.peran.org.uk/CelticChristianity.htm

www.painsley.org.uk

www.aidanandhilda.org.uk

www.lindisfarne-scriptorium.co.uk

www.newtara.org

www.northumbriacommunity.org

www.anamcharafellowship.org

www.irishchristian.org

www.independentcelticepiscopalchurch.org

www.celtic-circle.com

LATIMER PUBLICATIONS

GGC	God, Gays and the Church: Human Sexuality and Experience in Christian Thinking – eds. Lisa Nolland, Chris Sugden, Sarah Finch
WTL	The Way, the Truth and the Life: Theological Resources for a Pilgrimage to a Global Anglican Future – eds. Vinay Samuel, Chris Sugden, Sarah Finch
AEID	Anglican Evangelical Identity – Yesterday and Today – J.I.Packer and N.T.Wright
IB	The Anglican Evangelical Doctrine of Infant Baptism – John Stott and J.Alec Motyer
BF	Being Faithful: The Shape of Historic Anglicanism Today – Theological Resource Group of GAFCON
FWC	The Faith we confess: An exposition of the 39 Articles – Gerald Bray
TPG	The True Profession of the Gospel: Augustus Toplady and Reclaiming our Reformed Foundations – Lee Gatiss
SG	Shadow Gospel: Rowan Williams and the Anglican Communion Crisis – Charles Raven
TTB	Translating the Bible: From Willliam Tyndale to King James – Gerald Bray
PWS	Pilgrims, Warriors, and Servants: Puritan Wisdom for Today's Church – ed. Lee Gatiss
PPA	Preachers, Pastors, and Ambassadors: Puritan Wisdom for Today's Church – ed. Lee Gatiss
CWP	The Church, Women Bishops and Provision: The Integrity of Orthodox Objections to the Proposed Legislation Allowing Women Bishops

Lightning Source UK Ltd.
Milton Keynes UK
UKOW052322100212

187080UK00001B/53/P